life is simple;

we make it complicated

and complain we don't understand it.

'kanak'

let's uncomplicate it.

The Journey Of Life As I See

THE JOURNEY OF LIFE AS I SEE

dedicated to

THE SOURCE

and thanks to Pavan,
my partner in my current journey,
for her inspirations.

Subhash Gandhi

THE JOURNEY OF LIFE AS I SEE

by

Subhash Gandhi 'kanak'

A practical guide to
understanding
life
and its
simplicities

THE JOURNEY OF LIFE AS I SEE

By

Subhash Gandhi 'Kanak'

The views expressed in this book are based upon the author's personal experiences and the understanding of the topics herein. Resemblance if any, to any religion, faith or belief, is purely coincidental. This book is intended only for the general interest of the readers. The author and the publisher assume no responsibility for any conflicts, omissions or errors - potential or otherwise implied, and disclaim any liability arising directly or indirectly from the use of this book.

Published by: Shivdev Company Ltd.
24 Edinburgh Drive, Richmond Hill
Ontario, Canada L4B 1W3

Printed in Canada by Webcom.

First publication: 4,500 copies in paperback   June 2000

ISBN 0-9687109-0-5

Copies of this book may be ordered by calling 905-886-7454 or 905-883-8904 or by E-Mail: scgandhi@altavista.com or vngandhi@altavista.com

THE JOURNEY OF LIFE AS I SEE

Who am I?
What am I?
Where was I before I came 'here'?
What am I doing 'here'?
What and where is 'here'?
Who's breathing in me?
Who thinks and acts in me?
Where will I 'go' after death?
What can I take with me when I go?
What's real and what's not?
How to 'live' like a 'living being'
Where is the 'Creator'?
What's love?
What's life?

Based on the author's personal revelations, this book tries to explain the above and more, in simple terms.

Congratulations; You're on your way to experience what *life* is all about.

INDEX

A different you........139
A lost child.............121
Acceptance of the..... 9
All I need to do.........76
Allotted period of.... 55
Are we alone..............4
Are we listening.......13
Are we nuts..............48
Are you content.....129
Are you jealous........87
Are you really in.....117
Attchd, detch.unat...64
Awake or asleep........39
Baby - friend to all..114
Back to the Source...10
Be honest, you'll........98
Belief..........................93
Believe it or not........94
Bonds of selfishness..88
Box in a box..............47
Busy, busy - are we...63
Boredom is bliss........70
Conductor and the...21
Creation.....................5
Day or night..............34
Diplomacy.................96
Do good and good ...99
Do you have a goal..84
Do you know this.....12
Don't cry baby........123
Don't worry be........100
Dream or reality.......41
End is the beginning.77
Faith..........................95
Fear...........................132

Forgive me, please.. 61
Getting old are we..131
Give up what you.....67
Going, going, gone....46
Happy birthday.........56
Honesty is the best...97
How do we feel.........23
How do you live.......59
I love you, you love115
If I could only see.....27
Is this what I am.......24
Last day of my life....79
Let it be....................80
Let's get unattached.66
Life............................45
Living beings are.......35
Living in space..........42
Loneliness is not.......68
Lost and found.......124
Love is.....................110
Love, love, love......111
Love or duty...........109
Midlife crisis...........126
Nothing to do...........73
Out of this world......20
Passing time -are we.37
Past, present, future.33
Pride of ownership..105
Resting is not easy....71
Real need..................89
Should we have........86
So, what's new...........7
So, what's real...........40
Soul and the binder..26
Source of thoughts...22

Stop running...........137
Stop the world.........75
The bond...................25
The Creator.............. 8
The guide..................11
The light within......138
The righteousness.... 90
The root cause........104
The Source.................3
The truth hurts.......118
The urge to merge.. ..28
Toys playing with......60
Trains, planes, buses.51
Traveler, destination.19
To be or not to be.....52
True love.................113
True vs. untrue..........6
Want to live long......38
Wave and the ocean.53
We're a happy 112
What do we talk.....103
What is Karma........54
What is success.........83
What's in it for me....78
What's time..............36
Where is the Creator.16
Where's evil............116
Who is the Creator...15
Why are we unhappy49
Why do we argue......62
Why don't we get it128
Why me...................101
Will you make a......125

CONTENTS

Why this book?

How to get most out of this book?

1. Creator and Creation 1

2. What am I? 17

3. Time 31

4. Life - A Journey 43

5. How to Live 57

6. Life's Real Needs 81

7. Myths and Facts 91

8. What's Love? 107

9. The Paradox 119

10. Final Words 135

WHY THIS BOOK?

Over the years I have gone through numerous revelations about the life, its creation and complexities (or should I say, the simplicities) and its relationship to the Creator. When the urge to share these revelations exactly the way I have been exposed to, became overwhelming, I tried to put them in words, to the best of the ability I have been blessed with.

Whether you are a teenager or adult, in the prime of your life or at the twilight, you'll find this book of great assistance in unlocking the mysteries of this thing we call 'life'.

The book deals with life's non-material aspects as I see and I hope you will find the contents helpful in raising your awareness of the true values of life.

Good luck.

June 2000

Subhash Gandhi
Richmond Hill,
Ontario, Canada L4B 1W3
Tel. 905-886-7454
E Mail:
scgandhi@altavista.com

HOW TO GET
MOST OUT OF THIS BOOK

Dear reader,

It is recommended that you read only one chapter in one sitting. After completing a chapter, say 'How to live?', you may wish to close the book and ponder how the contents relate to your personal life.

Review the topic or topics you find most significant in the chapter and assess how it can be of benefit in your daily life. You may even have an urge to take some constructive action after reading a chapter. Don't hesitate, take the first step to make mends, if you feel inspired to do so.

After you've gone through the whole book, hopefully in many sessions, you'll perhaps develop your own technique to review the book on a regular basis and relate the contents to your own lifestyle.

The rewards are unending. All you have to do is, try.

Good luck.

The Author

chapter 1

CREATOR AND CREATION

What's in chapter 1

The Source
Are We Alone?
Creation
True vs. Untrue
So, What's New?
The Creator
Acceptance of the Source
Back to the Source
The Guide
Do you know this person?
Are We Listening?
Who 'is' the Creator?
Where 'is' the Creator?

THE SOURCE

I looked at the sunrise
And wondered who did that
I wondered at the high noon
And pondered at sunset.

Along came the darkness
With moon and the stars
Who is behind all this
With Sun, Jupiter and Mars.

There has to be someone sustaining,
Universe and its glow
It just can't happen by itself
Guess, who is running the SHOW.

kanak

ARE WE ALONE?

Should we care?

I sure don't.

We *are*, isn't that enough?

We waste too much time and energy in trying to justify, rationalize, or should I say, glorify, our existence, pretending to be something unique in this vast creation.

Wouldn't it really be a shock if we did find intelligent life on another planet?

What would that do to our ego; I'm not too sure.

Don't stop here, there's more.

CREATION

From the word 'Create'.

Create, To make or to cause to exist.

Everything - all that there 'is' - seen, unseen, felt, unfelt, realized, unrealized, invented yet or not, discovered, undiscovered - simply exists, has always existed and will always exist in some shape or form. Anything to be invented or to be discovered already exists; we simply do not know it yet.

What does the word research mean to you?

'Re' 'Search' - see what I mean?

TRUE VS. UNTRUE

It is true for now that you're reading this book and whatever you'll be doing after this, will also be true for that instant. What's true now will be replaced by what would appear to be true the next moment.

Not only that, sometimes what appears to be true may actually be camouflaged by the prevailing circumstances. The so-called knowledge, may change with *evolution* hence what appears to be true, may be so, only for as long as the validity of the current knowledge/perception, upholds in the mind of the observer.

What's true today may not be so tomorrow, or vice versa. Hence, rather than constantly *struggling to get to the bottom of everything*, wouldn't it be better to live and reconcile with each moment in life as it's being unfolded, without worrying too much about whether it's true or untrue?

SO, WHAT'S NEW?

Nothing is new. Whatever there is, has always existed, and will always exist, in some shape or form; whether, at the present time, we *know* it or not and whether it is *visible* or not.

Things simply change their shape, composition or form, resulting in *materials* of various properties.

And we call them *inventions or discoveries*, giving no consideration to the process, which propelled the thoughts to invent or to discover, into the mind of an *inventor or discoverer*, in the first place.

Remember the common phrase 'why didn't *I* think of that?'

Well, *why didn't you?*

Why someone else, *thought of that?*

THE CREATOR

If we did
What we think we did
Then who did
What we didn't do?

kanak

ACCEPTANCE OF THE SOURCE

My desire of accepting the Source, seems rather egoistic to me.

How can a drop of water absorb the ocean?

Even if I *do* eventually *find* the Source and *make It mine*; all I really would be doing is, preserving my egoistic 'I' while overshadowing the Source.

Doesn't make sense to me.

Hard to imagine, isn't it?

What should I be doing instead? Read on.

BACK TO THE SOURCE

If I am really looking for lasting peace, I have no choice but to go back to the Source.

Like a drop of water merging its 'own' identity, with the vast ocean by becoming part of it, in fact becoming the ocean itself.

And suddenly there are no worries, no anxieties and no misgivings about anything.

Surrendering to the Source, is what tranquility is all about.

THE GUIDE

The master, the guide, is one who, *with no personal interest, financial or otherwise,* is willing to share the knowledge of the realities of life; who, *without any compensation whatsoever,* trains and guides the pupil, to the appropriate path and upon successful completion of the training, leaves the pupil alone to walk the path and practice the *newfound skills.*

Such a guide or master, with a 'hands off approach', is never too far from the pupil, at various steps of the *learning process.* He or she may not be wearing a special robe, may not look charismatic, and may not even be very *educated or intellectual.* But you will find your guide if you seek sincerely. It's is closer than you think.

How will you recognize such a person? Look into his/her eyes and see how easily he/she delivers *the message.* You'll feel the radiance and warmth, the moment you meet such a person. What this person looks like, won't be important to you. Your mind will tell you that you want to be with and learn from that person. Don't let your ego come in your way. When you're sure, don't hesitate to surrender yourself to the training of this guide.

And if the guide finds you're the right candidate, he/she will share all his/her *wealth* with you with no strings attached. Then go ahead and *bask in bliss.*

DO YOU KNOW THIS PERSON?

We often meet people in life with whom, merely shaking hands or just saying hello, is a great pleasure. The smile and the body language of these people depict sincerity, love and care. Such people are around us but our ego prevents us from recognizing them.

These are the people who always have a serene smile, who burst with laughter and openly show their emotions and seem to take interest in whatever is going on around them. Too bad, rather than learning the art of life from them, we tend to put these people down. Their niceness gets labelled as being 'too nosy' and their unselfish act, as 'something hidden under the sleeve'.

Next time, when you meet such a person, greet him or her with a sincere, firm hand-shake and feel the blissful energy rushing through your entire system.

And once you get focussed with the characterstics of such a person, chances are that you will share the same enthusiasm with the next person *you meet*.

And what a great feeling that is!

ARE WE LISTENING?

Generally, we are very eager to criticize or find faults in someone who appears to be doing anything worthwhile, especially if it's someone we know. Admit it or not, we tend to believe negative things about people without too much convincing but we find hard to accept their good things; we want proof and even after that we may or may not accept. Why is that?

There is an inherent human tendency to be better than everyone else. Right from childhood, we are prompted to defeat others and be number one. The whole society is geared towards competitiveness. Obviously, when we find someone who is better than us in anything, our ego overtakes our judgement and we begin analyzing and tearing apart the virtues that made that person better than us.

Whenever certain genuine people tried to share their knowledge of seeking the 'truth of life', they were shunned, crucified, burnt alive, poisoned, beheaded or were kept *quiet* by other means. The reason was simple, those in power felt that their supremacy was being challenged and they would lose their authority if such a person was allowed to survive.

The irony however, is that the same people after

destroying such great individuals, promoted the same views which those great personalities were trying to present in the first place. Why, one may ask.

The simple answer is that once this special person is gone, the implied threat of him or her taking over the power from the so-called followers, is also gone. The teachings may still be followed in one form or the other but the person who started the whole thing in the first place, is no longer present, *to boss the followers around.* Many *followings* in this world, flourished only after the master had passed away. The real message however, remained undelivered or unexplained in many cases.

Let's not make the same mistake. Let's pay attention when someone special is trying to share with us 'the secrets of life'. We know, not much has worked so far. If it had, we would all be permanently at peace; everyone would have followed one path and would have been happy. On the contrary, there is more misery, mistrust and tension now than ever before.

Are we making sincere effort to find, recognize and follow such a person?

WHO 'IS' THE CREATOR?

Wrong question!

Does it really matter?

Will it change anything if I knew who or what the Creator is? Will the realization, that there *is* a creator for all I can see, hear and feel, change anything in my life? Will I become a better person or will I just gloat about my *new found knowledge*?

I don't see any need to fuss about who created our solar system, the galaxy, or even the entire universe for that matter. The reality is, that I'm here and I must make the best use of my *being here*.

Many feel, everything is just one or the other form of 'energy' manifested in a material shape that can be seen, heard, touched or felt; sort of energy manifesting itself in other forms of *material energy*.

And if the Creator itself is nothing but a vast source of energy, so be it.

I have no problem with that.

WHERE 'IS' THE CREATOR?

Wrong question again.

It's like asking where's heat in the sun or fragrance in the flower?

All over my friend, in every speck of whatever there is - in earth, water, air, fire and space. Although not visible to the naked eye, the Creator's presence can be felt in the entire creation just like heat in the sun and fragrance in the flower. It's probably fair to say that the heat and the sun are one and the same thing and so are the fragrance and the flower because it's almost impossible to perceive one without the other.

The 'truth' is that the Creator is manifest in every little spec of dust, earth, water, fire, air, space and all that's seen or unseen, felt or unfelt, realized or unrealized. All that there 'is' is therefore, the Creator itself.

Creator, Creation, Creativity and the Creatures; all in one and one in all.

How wonderful!

chapter 2

WHAT AM I?

What's in chapter 2

Traveler and Destination
Out of this world
Conductor and the Driver
Source of Thoughts
How do We feel?
Is This What I am?
The Bond
Soul and the Binder
If I Could Only See Me
The Urge to Merge

TRAVELER AND
DESTINATION

'I' the soul
using the body
as my vehicle
travel through
the journey of various lives
to reach my ultimate goal
to merge with
The Source
'I' originally came from.

That's 'me'!

kanak

OUT OF THIS WORLD

or any world as a matter of fact

'I' the soul
am in transit
in this material world
travelling through
various 'life cycles'
with the ultimate goal
that is
reaching my 'final home'
which is
out of this material world
                                          kanak

CONDUCTOR
AND
THE DRIVER

'I', the soul, the traveler in the vehicle called my body, am also it's conductor. But the driver, you guessed it right, the mind, with it's three powerful assistants - intellect, obsession and ego, generally tends to be a deterrent in completing each journey as planned.

These four keep diverting my attention to the trivial matters such as material success, lust, anger, jealously possessiveness, pride of ownership, winning at all costs etc. etc.

'I', the conductor, must keep the driver under control and not allow it to wander. In order to reach my final destination promptly, I must keep the driver focussed on the destination.

SOURCE OF THOUGHTS

To me, my brain appears to be only a relay center - not the originator of the thoughts, like an electrical substation channeling electricity to various points, to cause action. The *power* in fact, is being fed by the *operator* of the generating station , as directed by the *owner*.

Does body, mind and soul sound familiar?

Mind (ever so clever and materially oriented), receives thoughts from the soul and channels them to the brain with or without some 'material' modification. The brain then directs the body accordingly.

At least that's what I think, *thinking* is all about.

What do *you* think?

HOW DO WE FEEL?

A sensation at any part of the body gets transmitted to the brain, which passes it on to the mind. It is the mind's choice to ignore or pass judgement on the sensation or seek guidance from the soul prior to passing the judgement

The mind, being obsessed with the material world, generally tends to ignore the soul and generates a *reaction* relying upon it's peers - the intellect, obsession and the ego; and not necessarily the way it really ought to be.

We feel (or hear or see) what our mind wants us to.

IS THIS WHAT I AM?

A composite of physical body (made of five gross material elements - earth, water, air, fire, space) attached to a spiritual entity (Soul) via four materio-spiritual elements Mind, Intellect, Obsession and Ego herewith referred to as the 'binder'.

The physical body - conceived by the union of two body fluids, becomes a 'living being' when a spiritual entity - the soul, attaches itself to the body thru the 'binder'

The physical body grows with the nourishment from the five gross material elements. The mind who has a mind of it's own, controls actions of the body with or without the guidance of the soul. Poor body! Stuck between the mind and the soul.

THE BOND

I, the soul
being a non-material entity
am bonded
to the material body
with
Mind, Intellect,
Obsession and Ego

kanak

All four are clearly evident by how the body behaves in this material world.

You cannot see the mind, intellect, obsession and ego but you can notice their existence in the way you conduct yourself. They make you feel like *somebody*, don't they?

SOUL AND THE BINDER

The soul's sole function is to prepare itself for the ultimate dissolution into where it came from - The Source.

The binder's function is exactly what the name suggests - to keep the soul 'bound' to the material world.

The binder is very powerful. It has four strong soldiers always working towards preventing the soul to reach its goal. Let's see how this happens:

M. MIND - the chief: germinates seeds of desire.
I. INTELLECT: mostly justifies it, rarely nullifies.
O. OBSESSION: plans action to fulfill the desire.
E. EGO: prompts the mind for more when a desire is fulfilled. Upon failure, the ego prompts the mind to look for other alternatives.

BEWARE OF THE M.I.O.E. EFFECT

The poor soul all by itself, has an uphill battle against the 'big four'. To achieve its goal, the soul has to constantly struggle with the mind, to keep germinating the thoughts of unattachment. Not an easy task, I must say.

IF I COULD ONLY SEE ME

Without the mirror that is.

When we become able to watch our 'self' performing in life, from a distance, becoming a *witness* to all our actions, we can then, *see* the uselessness of the majority of the things in our daily life. We would then be able to see the insignificance of the material wealth, relations, friends, enemies and many other things we thought were important.

Many things which we thought were our assets, would then appear to be the liabilities. Being a witness would enable us to weed out the liabilities from the real assets and we'll then, be able to focus on our journey to the final destination.

Impossible! You say? I don't think so.

Living but not being *possessed* by life; enjoying life but not being attached to it - like fish living in water but not getting 'wet'; is the key to being your own 'witness'.

THE URGE TO MERGE

One of the most significant features of this planet seems to be the tendency to go back to the original natural state. Anything, which has been modified or changed to any other shape, composition or form, tends to somehow retrace the journey to its origin.

The fruits, the flowers and even the trees eventually go back to where they came from - the earth. Most of the metals mined and extracted forms the ores eventually find their way back to the form they were originally extracted from. Even the so-called indestructible products are supposed to have a life cycle. All living beings eventually *die* reverting the *material body* back to the original five gross elements i. e. earth, water, air, fire and space.

Water rising from the ocean in the form of vapors, changes to clouds, rains back onto the earth and eventually finds it way back to the ocean through streams and rivers.

Various gravitational forces in the universe constantly work to pull all they can, towards their centers. Everything seems to journey back to the source regardless of the number of *life cycles* it has to go through.

The occupier of the body, 'the soul' is no different. It also has a constant urge to go back to the Source and the 'human life cycle' seems to be the the most rational stage towards developing this ability. Everyone, in his own way, via different paths, is after the same goal - 'permanent peace and happiness' with no fear or anxieties.

Our ego may not let us accept this, but in reality we all are looking for lasting contentment which I feel, is only possible when we become *one* with the Source.

And that oneness is only achievable when we become unattached to the consequences of our actions.

Urge to merge - a universal concept.

chapter 3

TIME

What's in chapter 3

Past, Present and Future
Day or Night
Living Beings - Are We?
What's Time?
Passing Time, Are We?
Want to Live Long?
Dreaming or Awake?
So, What's Real?
Dream or Reality?
Living in Space

PAST, PRESENT AND FUTURE

Present is nothing but future turning into past. The moment we say "It's 3.01 P.M." it's already passed; the next minute has already begun. The statement "He's twenty years old" actually means that the person is more than twenty because the twentieth birthday has long past.

Anything we see at any moment, actually changes by the time we realize that we have seen it, regardless of how miniscule the *realization time* may be.

Everything either *was* or *will be*, in some shape or form. But the Creator who is present in everything that exists, always *is*; there is no question of was or will be. The Creator simply *is* - with or without any creation - omnipresent and beyond time.

Photographs taken by various spacecrafts, have shown continuous formation and destruction of stars and galaxies, thousands of light years away. 'Some power' let's call it the Creator, has to be responsible for what's going on *out there and here* as a matter of fact.

Our pride, ego and obsession with the outward scenario prevent us to see wood for the trees, ocean for the waves and Creator for the Creation.

DAY OR NIGHT

For an optimist,
a night is a short break between two days.

For a pessimist,
a day is an interruption between two nights.

What does a day mean to you?

Is your day an interruption in darkness
or
A sunny continuance with minor shade?

LIVING BEINGS - ARE WE?

'Living while being' - what a beautiful phrase!

Note 'ing' in the title; LIVING - the continuity, the passing of time during the journey of life.

And what seems to be the requirement for passing the said time? BEING - what else?

But what do we really do? Do we really pass the said time by *being* what we are or by *doing* what we 'want to do'? The latter, I am sure. We seem to want to make changes and control everything and everyone around us.

Our false sense of power and ego makes us forget the real purpose of life, which is simply 'being what we are' and not pretending to be someone or something we are not.

Living being in my definition therefore, is an entity which should be living by being what it really is.

We can be true *living beings* if we simply *let it be*.

Think about it.

WHAT'S TIME?

Have you ever wondered about what the 'time' really is?

Let's see. From the many definitions of time, to me, the most appropriate one seems to be 'an allotted period of life'.

And this allotted period is measured in years, days, hours and so on. When this time is over for any particular 'thing' or 'being', it's life is over too. No matter what we may have possessed or achieved in life, nothing will matter to us when the *time's up*.

Is the entire running around in life therefore, really worth it?

Time keeps on flowing like a river taking in everybody and everything with it, when the allotted period of life for any entity, is over.

Simply put, Time owns yesterday, today and tomorrow, Time owns everything and rules on everything, *period*.

Remember the old saying 'Time and tide wait for none'?

PASSING TIME, ARE WE?

Seems about right. Since the life cycle is just an allotted period of time for each individual; each day, hour or minute just indicates that a portion of the allotted time has been depleted. And no matter what, when the *time's up*, everything achieved during the lifetime will have to be left here. The party i.e. the worldly dream, will be over.

Aren't we simply passing time regardless of what we do?

All our actions, anything we say, think or do, have one thing in common - we're passing time in the process.

If we all have the same objective of our *being here*, wouldn't it make sense to be in harmony with our co-existents and surroundings?

Since everything has an allotted period of life and then changes it's shape or form, does it make any sense in being possessive of what we have or even what we are?

Remember 'Existence is eternal, Existent is not'.

WANT TO LIVE LONG?

How long do you want to live? Eighty, ninety, one hundred, two hundred years? Maybe forever?

How long you think you can *enjoy* life if you never fell sick, were always young and rich?

Do you know it is not uncommon to become bored with riches, sex, fame and other so called *pleasures*? We often hear about the depression of rich and famous. Do you think that all the rich and famous are happy with their lives?

No matter how good a life is, when it becomes routine, it becomes boring and that's when one looks for change. Child wants to be youth, youth wants to be an adult and the adults eventually, start wondering what lies ahead. Almost everyone, at some point in life, wonders about what's beyond death.

Changes are inevitable and the desire for change is the inherent characteristic of human beings. We may wish to live forever but we can't stop the clock, can we? Remember, *if our wish for immortality comes true, we may be stuck to live with it for a very long time.*

What's my point you say? *You* figure it out.

AWAKE OR ASLEEP?

That's all we really go through in our entire life cycle. We are either awake or asleep - with dreams being an integral part of either state, mostly while we're asleep.

While in dream, everything appears real - the place, the people, the happenings. It is only when we are *awake* we find all that happened in the dream, was false. The dream in fact, appears so real that if, someone within the dream itself, tried to warn us that what's happening is not real, we would probably refuse to listen to that person and would go on enjoying the dream or living the nightmare as the case might be.

Let's talk about our *current awake state*. We know that when a dream is over, the *awakened state* clearly suggests that the dream was unreal, a non-event when compared to the *awake state*; a figment of our imagination. Likewise, when our *current awake state* is over, I mean after completion of the current life cycle, could there be another state that may again suggest that all what happened in this life cycle, was also a dream?

Are we paying attention to someone who's trying to tell us so? Is this 'material' world as 'unreal' as the dreams are?

Is there a real world *out there*?

SO, WHAT'S REAL?

Actual state of being or existence is what makes anything 'real'. The irony however is that whatever appears to exist today, may not exist tomorrow in its present form. As a matter of fact whatever is in front of us at any particular moment is not the same a moment later although it may seem to be the same. The creation, along with its shape and contents is constantly changing except of course for the Creator who is invisible to the physical eye but is omnipresent.

So, is our own body real? Are our thoughts real? What about our surroundings, our friends, relatives, our children? Are they real? Aren't we all *here today, gone tomorrow*?

Does anything stay like it is now, forever? Even this body I call as mine, is not real in the *real* sense of the word since it changes continuously and eventually *dies*. And by the way, *what really happens to me when I am no more*?

Let's get real, Okay?

DREAM OR REALITY?

How often have you felt a *live reaction* to a dream or nightmare? Anxiety, fear, sweating, fast heartbeat or certain other physical reactions are not uncommon during or immediately after a dream. Many wake up screaming after a nightmare.

If a dream is just that, a 'dream', then why does one feel a reaction of a dream in this so called 'real world'? Could it be that either the dream itself is a reality or this so-called real world itself is a dream? One thing is for sure; the happenings of one realm do have a cause and effect in the other realm. What do you think?

And about true reality, only those who know about the existence before birth or after death, know for sure. And even if you knew, how would you explain it to someone who doesn't understand the 'language'? I'm talking about that special 'channel' and the 'decoder' that lies within, waiting to get 'activated'.

As far as the life is concerned, our pride and ego, based on our *current knowledge and tools*, prevent us from knowing *the reality*. It is not uncommon to label a *realized person* 'crazy' if his/her behavior pattern doesn't fit the current norms of the society - mostly because the society is not able to relate to the actions of such a person. Pity.

LIVING IN SPACE?

Where do we live? In a house or in an apartment, in a hut or in a mobile home? Think again.

Aren't we living in *space*? We build four walls, a floor and a roof within the open space and call it our home. Not only that, we build walls within the walls, homes within homes, to 'protect' ourselves from the *space* from which there's no escape. There is space inside the home and space outside, all part and parcel of the same entity. The only visible barriers are simply man-made; remove them and all appears the same once again – open, wide space. It had never changed in the first place; only looked so.

The earth, water, air and fire, all are part and parcel of the same entity - space. It is also ironic therefore, that the barriers, which are supposed to isolate us from the space, are made from the material taken from the space itself.

In fact, we're using space to separate ourselves from the space.

Wow!

chapter 4

LIFE'S
A JOURNEY

What's in chapter 4

Life
Going... Going... Gone
Box in a Box in a...
Are We Nuts?
Why are We Unhappy?
Trains, Planes and Buses
To be or Not to be
Wave and the Ocean
What is Karma?
Allotted Period of Life
Happy Birthday

LIFE

A period during which anything continues to exist in its current state.

For creatures that would be a state in which its organs are capable of performing their functions. But let's be serious, isn't life more than just functioning of some organs?

What do *you* think life is?

Life is a sequence of events that happen during the period elapsed between the birth and the death of a living being; note the word 'happen'.

We call our successes as our 'doing', but we generally refer to our failures as 'happenings'; how sad! Well, my friend, if our failures are 'happenings' then so are our successes; all planned and predetermined - like it or not, believe it or not.

Life is what goes on.

And when the ongoing ceases, the vehicle that carried the life, is deceased.

Something to think about.

GOING... GOING... GONE.

And suddenly at a predetermined moment and in a preplanned fashion, the life is *gone* from the material body which I so proudly used to refer to as *my body*.

No more 'I' and no more *my body*.

The body is buried or cremated but whatever happens to 'I', is another story.

BOX IN A BOX IN A...

Trying to understand life is like opening a box, finding another one, opening that one, finding another and so on.

A lifetime is spent just doing this, in curiosity, rather than simply enjoying each moment as it is being unfolded in front of us.

We wait for or keep trying for specific things to happen but do not stop to really 'be with' whatever is around us. And what a wonderful experience that is - ask those who are 'with it'.

Does the phrase 'Oh, get with it' ring a bell?

ARE WE NUTS?

NUT. A fruit or legume with an edible core inside a hard shell.

The core creates a hard shell around it, hoping to be secure from destruction but the inevitable does happen and the barrier, eventually breaks. The core loses its physical identity by rotting, by being crushed or by being gobbled up with or without the hard shell.

Perhaps that's why irrational people, are sometimes referred to as *nuts* by their colleagues.

Our miseries and pains often occur due to our non-acceptance of the failures - the negatives that are inter-twined with the positives.

Acceptance of life but not death, happiness but not sadness, success but not the failure and praise but not the insult - is only a partial acceptance of the 'life system' and that's what makes us unhappy, miserable and resentful.

Most of us do not learn to 'accept' the negatives and spend most of our lifetime, in vain, creating a *shell of security* to protect us from the obvious and inevitable.

Are we 'nuts'?

WHY ARE WE UNHAPPY?

The reason we are generally unhappy is because we expect everything to be favorable or good in our life. We're just not willing to accept things as they are, *good or bad*.

To exist, a coin must have two opposite sides. Similarly, there has to be an 'opposite' side of everything that exists, like black for white, dark for bright, night for day, negative for positive etc. etc.

The prefix 'un' denotes exactly the opposite. For every condition to be valid therefore, the 'un' i.e. the opposite condition has to exist, otherwise there will be no balance and the whole system will fall apart.

For every favorable condition therefore, there has to be an unfavorable one though one may not necessarily follow right after the other; especially when a series of one type of happening are taking place - *good or bad*. Rest assured, that once a string of one type is over, the opposite will materialize.

Our problem is that we fail to realize this universal truth. We simply want everything to be well in our life and the moment something goes wrong we become miserable wondering why we *deserved it*.

The secret of permanent happiness therefore lies in the

understanding that things *will go wrong* at certain times in our lives and we must accept them the same way we accept good things.

Like it or not, we really have no choice in this matter.

If we can't beat them why not join them?

Let's learn to accept the unfavorable conditions the same way as we accept the favorable ones, without asking any questions.

Try it; life from hereon will become simple and easy to 'live with'.

TRAINS, PLANES AND BUSES

While traveling, we may appear attached to our seats, the surroundings and our fellow travelers but on completion of the journey, we normally leave the vehicle unattached and go onwards.

Our journey of life via the vehicle of the 'material' body is no different.

However, most of us generally live in the fear of losing our possessions, relatives, friends *and* our prestige. This is mainly due to our bonds of selfishness and pride of ownership.

To understand life's virtues, we need to realize that on completion of our current journey through this material world, these 'trains, planes, buses, companions and *the route itself*', will be of no future value to the traveler - the soul.

And when this realization occurs, the journey of life becomes smooth and pleasant.

TO BE OR NOT TO BE

'Doing good' is an action, which has an inherent expectation of results. It may be a reward of some kind or just a good feeling. And that makes a person, bound or attached, to the action taken.

The *doing good feeling* therefore, can also bring misery to *the doer* if the results of the *doing good*, do not turn out as expected.

'Being good' on the other hand, is a state - a condition that's natural. One doesn't have to do anything to *be good* because if you *are* good, you won't do bad things, period. And there won't be an expectation of results either.

A person in the state of 'being good' therefore, performs good deeds all of the time, *au natural*, but is totally unattached to the results of his/her actions.

Such a person is free from all anxieties and fears.

WAVE AND THE OCEAN

A wave, emerging from the ocean, is nothing but an extension of the ocean itself. It is always attached to the ocean and after a while merges back into where it came from. At any given instant, simultaneously, countless waves emerge, grow, shrink and merge into the ocean at different times. A novice observer can only see the waves and not the ocean.

Outwardly, it is almost impossible even for the wave to see its origin and eventual dissolution into the ocean because it is surrounded by millions of other waves. A wave can easily get 'lost' or distracted in the world of young, old, birthing and dying multitude of waves. Amidst this confusion, the ocean becomes obscure and the waves fall into the trap of believing the 'world of waves' as the real world.

The *enlightened* outside observer, however, *knows* that each and every wave eventually merges back into the ocean. Most waves re-emerge several times in various shapes or forms but eventually do merge back into its source - the vast, peaceful ocean.

To me, the life is nothing more than a wave, with the ultimate goal to merge with the Source.

WHAT IS KARMA?

Many do not believe in Karma and feel each person's destiny is in his/her own hands. You may be one of those who attribute your successes to *your* hard work; but what about those who worked as hard, even harder but did not succeed? What do *you* have which *they* don't?

If everything is supposed to be the result of what we do *in this life* then what do we specifically 'do' to deserve certain diseases such as cancer? What did the embryo do to be born autistic, blind or otherwise handicapped? If it is due to something the parents did then why does the infant have to bear the consequences? Why the child should suffer if only the parents are to be *punished*?

Why someone is a fantastic painter, singer or a hockey player while others cannot be as good no matter how hard they try? Why someone is exceedingly beautiful or ugly, tall or short, genius or retarded? What did these persons do to be what they are? Why do DNA and genes behave the way they do?

Perhaps the seeds sown in previous lives are bearing fruit in this life. May be the previous Karma are coming home to roost.

How disturbing!

ALLOTTED PERIOD OF LIFE?

Like the 'shelf life' of a 'manufactured item', the lifetime of each 'being' is predetermined, pre-allotted before it is put on the 'shelf' of this material world.

Allotted by who? Who decides how much time one will live, and where and why?

And by the way, *who* really lives in the body for the said allotted time anyway? *Who or what* leaves the body when we say so and so is gone?

Upon death, the entire body looks the same as it was before, though the organs may not be functioning anymore; so *who is gone* and *where*?

When we say, 'so and so is no more', what do we really mean? Doesn't the use 'is' with 'no more', sound paradoxical?

Does the word 'soul' make any sense at this juncture?

HAPPY BIRTHDAY!

A birthday is just a reminder that I have used one more year of the allotted time in this life cycle.

Have I passed the time in the past year wisely or just wasted it in the trivial attachments with this material world?

I must review today what I'll be doing during the next year to ensure that I have utilized my *allotted time* in the most appropriate manner, *to fulfill* my current journey on this planet.

Will I be able to say next year, 'happy birthday to me' and be really 'happy' about it?

Will I 'let it be' or will I do it 'my way'?

chapter 5

HOW TO LIVE?

What's in chapter 5

How do 'You' live?
'Toys' Playing with Toys
Forgive Me, Please!
Why do We Argue So Much
Busy, Busy - are We?
Attached, Detached or Unattached
Let's Get Unattached
Give up What You Don't Have
Loneliness is Not a Curse
Boredom is Bliss!
Resting is Not Easy
Nothing to do!
Stop the World
All I Need to do
End is the Beginning
What's in it for Me?
Last Day of My Life
Let It Be?

HOW DO 'YOU' LIVE?

Living the life without zeal and passion is like a student reluctantly doing his homework; doing, because he has no choice. But those who do the homework with enthusiasm, with a keen desire to gain the knowledge and face the challenge, do well and are happy and comfortable with the education they are going through. This eventually leads them to professional success. Such people generally enjoy everything they do and are envy of those who can't.

If we face every moment with passion and courage, whether the situation is favorable or otherwise, we'll find that our mind remains clear and our body full of energy.

Let's not forget, we do not knows for sure if we will take the next breath or not. If we just do everything with a thought in mind that we are doing it for the last time because we don't know if there will be a next time, we would tend to put all our heart into it.

Every action would then become a pleasure and not a 'chore', whether we'd be working, playing, cooking, eating, singing, mowing lawn or just plain walking.

And that would mean no tension, no stress and a desire to live each day to it's fullest. And by the way, isn't this what life's all about?

'TOYS' PLAYING WITH TOYS

Like it or not, we seem to be nothing more than simple toys playing in the hands of a power which is far, far superior than us. We are insignificant, helpless entities in the vast scheme of the nature, universe and the entire creation.

We cannot even control the most significant function of our body; our own breathing. We live on materials created by who knows 'Who'. Our mere existence is not even under our control.

Yet, we move, talk, laugh, cry and perform most tasks in our lives, according to the individual *destiny*, for which each of us appears to have been 'programmed'. Very little, if any, is really in our hands. Are we 'toys' or what?

Oh yes, we do alter a few materials in format, style and composition for our 'convenience' and pretend to 'play' with them during our life cycle.

'Toys' playing with toys?

FORGIVE ME, PLEASE!

When we know there isn't much in our hands, and that we all kind of move like a puppet on a string, then why do we spend so much time and energy in judging other people and even ourselves? Why can't we just take the events of this life as the *happenings* and not as the deliberate attempts of other people trying to throw us off-track?

Our ego would almost certainly want us to *react* to various 'situations' that occur in our daily lives. But if we learn to accept things 'as they are' and not as they 'appear to be' or 'as we want them to be', we wouldn't then have to worry about the consequences, would we?

Forgiving brings instant peace of mind if we *forgive from the bottom of our heart*, with no strings attached.

Next time when you are disturbed because someone gave you hard time, try to forgive that person *from your heart*. You'll be amazed how good you feel.

Remember, it is not important whether the other person reciprocates; don't even expect it.

Contentment is the order of the day when you walk on this one-way street. Good luck.

WHY DO WE ARGUE SO MUCH?

Simply because we're afraid of being labeled as 'ignorant'. Whether we know the subject or not, we hasten to offer our 'expert' opinion on any matter, sometimes without even being asked.

The one who really *knows* may hesitate in giving his opnion. He may offer his views based on his own experiences but not present them as a show of his intelligence.

The 'know it all' on the other hand, will waste no time in showing how 'brilliant' he is and why everyone should just listen to him, shutting off the one who really knows.

The result! Loud and confusing opinions reign over the 'situation', obscuring the reality.

There is no shortage of the so-called leaders to the path of reality but the real knowledge and the capability to *deliver* it, belongs only to a chosen few.

Thank your lucky stars and don't let go of such a person, if and when you find one.

BUSY, BUSY - ARE WE?

Almost everyone appears to be busy these days doing something or the other. Being 'busy' is not only a way of life anymore, it has become an obsession. The biggest dilemma seems to be what to do after retirement. Well, why retire at all, if one still has to worry about what to do after retirement? Why are we so obsessed with 'doing things' instead of just 'being' what we are?

We become miserable if we have 'nothing to do'. I think it's because when our body and mind, both, are 'not busy', we begin to embark upon the journey to learn who we really are.

But not being used to see the 'self' from a distance, we become queasy, frustrated and disoriented, even scared and go back to the 'busy' world to distant ourselves from the reality. Unable to see and experience the 'reality' with our 'conscious' mind, we get scared and reinstall ourselves in the hustle and bustle of our routine lifestyle.

Obsession to the 'busyness' is just an escape from reality. Rather than running away from the 'empty mind' let's look deeper into the 'self' and explore what we really are.

Realization of the bliss, associated with an 'empty mind', is incredible.

ATTACHED, DETACHED OR UNATTACHED

Whether we're *attached with* or *detached from* something or someone, the emotional response in both cases is the same - anxiety, frustration, pride, fear of losing what we have or what we believe in etc. etc.

Sometimes we also become *attached* to the desire of what we don't even have and preoccupy our mind with the thoughts of fulfilling that desire.

Being *detached* from something is also a kind of attachment because now we're *attached* to the ego associated with the *detachment*. 'Oh, I don't do this anymore or that or I have nothing to do with such and such matter or person or I have quit such and such habit' etc. etc. These expressions actually show that we're still *attached* , only the mode has changed from physical to mental.

So what can we do for the lasting peace of mind? If by wanting, trying to get, having and giving up don't work then what's the remedy for the miseries in life?

The answer in fact, is so simple that we just don't care for it.

It's also, so easy, that most of us think that it won't work and therefore, we hesitate to even try it.

The answer lies in becoming *unattached* to everything - our desires, actions, emotions, likes and dislikes - like a person walking through a mall from one end to other, being fully aware of the shops, the products, the 'sales' and the temptation to buy, but leaving the mall without buying anything.

Shopping without buying. What a neat idea!

Remember, being *attached* or *detached*, both demand action which in turn generates reaction and hence, the emotional turbulence.

Being *unattached* on the other hand, makes one free from the emotional see-saw allowing one to go through life's journey rather smoothly.

LET'S GET UNATTACHED

Getting *unattached* does not mean not caring, loving or sharing. It only eliminates the emotions that are associated with the actions or the thoughts of possessiveness or deprivation.

Unattachment simply means not being obsessed with all those things, which we think matter to us. The pride of ownership in the 'attachment mode' and the sense of ego in the 'detachment mode', lead only to misery, because there is a risk of losing face, in the event of a failure, in either mode. The emotions come into play whether one is 'getting on the wagon' or 'falling off it'. The solution would then be, not to get involved with the 'wagon' in the first place.

Unattachment does not mean *indifference* either. It refers to being *aware* but not getting *obsessed*. It means, do what you have to but don't let the actions or the expectation of the results, run your life. Done is done and gone is gone, what has happened cannot be changed.

The real problem lies in the attachment to the process of the action and to the impending results. Doing what needs to be done 'without prejudice' and being immune to the consequences is what *unattachment* is all about.

GIVE UP WHAT YOU DON'T HAVE

Sounds odd, doesn't it?

If we're obsessed with a desire to possess something, then we have already taken the first step to acquire it. This promotes action, resulting in it's fulfillment or failure.

The fufillment elevates the ego and generates additional desires starting the *desire cycle* all over again; the failure brings frustration intensifying the original desire even more. One is never satisfied in either situation.

It's normal to have desires but if we can give up the obsession towards it's fulfillment before even getting involved, we won't have to worry about the consequences, would we?

Getting fed up with what we already have and then giving it up is not abnormal once we realize the insignificance of our material possessions but the real peace of mind is only possible when we are able to 'give up' our obsession to possess.

Giving up what we don't have, will therefore enhance *unattachment*, thus bringing us closer to our ultimate goal, merging with the Source.

LONELINESS IS NOT A CURSE

Contrary to what most of us may think of loneliness, it can be very useful if we are able to realize and harvest it's potential and benefits.

Like boredom, the feeling of loneliness, is also a reminder of the separation of our true identity, from the Source - our 'home' where we originally came from. Let's review this.

For a long time now, there has been a general consensus that the creation and the living beings are the material manifestation of some paranormal element. Our ego just doesn't let us admit this.

Remember the phrase 'so and so has passed away' - what do we mean by that? In a vague manner, we are kind of admitting that although the physical body is still visible, it's 'the occupant' who has completed his passing through this material world and has gone away. Gone where; we don't know, but we all feel sometimes that there is more to the life and death.

Feeling uncomfortable during loneliness is normal due to our lack of understanding as to what life is all about. In fact, these are the wonderful moments during which the memory of our real 'home' - our real relationship to the Source, is being refreshed in our mind. We are in fact, being warned about the fallacy of this material world and about the instability of all that surrounds us.

Our discomfort during loneliness will disappear if we're able to channel our thoughts towards understanding the true reasoning behind why we are feeling lonely in the first place.

Wouldn't it be great if we can find someone who can help us harvest the *energy* of loneliness and its virtues? I know from personal experience that if our quest is genuine, such a person is never far off. All we need is a keen desire to learn; and the guidance will be made available to us in due time. We must not give up.

It works; really!

BOREDOM IS BLISS!

Ever thought why we get bored sometimes?

When we are bored, everything around us appears insignificant. There seems no purpose in life, no point in doing anything. Why's that?

If the mind is constantly thinking and analyzing, then why all of a sudden it draws a *total blank*? If there is 'so much to do and so little time' then why do we get 'bored' in the first place. Why do we feel restless, lonely, nervous and afraid when we're in the 'bored mode'?

Boredom in fact, is a reminder of greater needs in life, a reminder of the separation of our true identity, from the Source. It's the yearning of the subconscious, to understand who we really are, where we came from and where we have to 'go' from here?

Instead of harvesting the energy of an *empty mind*, to explore our inner-self, we try to counteract the boredom by deliberately making ourselves *busy* in 'something or the other'. We try to get rid of boredom as if it was a curse.

What a waste!

RESTING IS NOT EASY

Nothing appears to be at rest, at any time. Even the things that appear unmoving, are really not still. The passengers or objects in a moving train may appear still to each other but to an outsider the train and it's contents appear to be moving at a fast speed.

We on this planet while appearing to be still, are in fact revolving around the axis of the earth at the speed of thousands of miles per hour. Not only that, the earth itself while turning around its own axis every twenty-four hours, also travels around our sun, at incredible speed. Our complete solar system also appears to be revolving around another system and so on.

Even the trees, the walls, roads, stones, anything that appears to be resting, are also always in motion within themselves or relative to their surroundings. The rivers flowing, the winds blowing, the clouds, the rain, the falls; all are reminder of things constantly in motion. Anything and everything - moving or otherwise is made of elements consisting of atoms, around the core of which, tiny electrons are moving at an incredible speed. A small bowl of yogurt has countless bacteria running around while the bowl and it's contents may appear still.

A sleeping person may seem resting but his thoughts may

be running wild culminating in dreams, where the mind is constantly in motion. The vital organs are continuously performing their function day and night; the heart continuously beating, the nose constantly breathing and the blood flowing tirelessly through blood vessels. The whole system is in motion all the time even though the body may seem at rest. Even at death, various components of the body, in fact *die* at different speeds.

Then how can we really rest? How can we be at rest or at peace with ourselves while so much commotion is going on? It appears there is no rest even after death so what should we do to achieve everlasting peace or restfulness.

Oh, we *have* developed certain 'norms' for peace and order in our lives, but do they really work? If they do, then why haven't we been able to live in harmony with our fellow beings? Why is there still so much misery on this planet? Why does everyone seem to be chasing one dream or the other? Why are the masses still unhappy even though many of their desires are constantly getting fulfilled?

The answer is clear but the veil of our pride and ego does not let us see the *truth*. The *truth is within* us, all we have to do is, take a deep dive within ourselves, with the help of a proper guide, to find the niche of lasting contentment.

And those who know the *truth*, just know it, that's all.

NOTHING TO DO!

How wonderful!

But are you sure you're doing nothing? Not physically maybe but isn't your mind running around all over the place? Isn't something bothering you or making you restless? If so, then you *are* doing something even though you may outwardly appear calm and unoccupied.

Even the thought of nothing to do is an action in itself.

All thoughts are generated by mind's action, waiting to manifest.

What's my point you say? Read on.

Sometimes, when the physical body is not performing any outward function and the mind ceases to generate any thoughts for a while, a sudden awareness of loneliness creeps up in the conscious mind. You know the queasy feeling I'm talking about.

Instead of worrying about such a feeling, we should be grateful because we have been awarded an opportunity to ponder over the real purpose of life. Only at these times we can rationally think about what we should be doing to prepare for the final journey of becoming one with our originator - the Source.

We cannot escape from this reality and unless we come to grips with this fact, we'll keep on roaming aimlessly, trying to *keep busy*, avoiding the truth and wondering why aren't we happy.

When I have nothing to do, I just sit comfortably in a not too bright place, close my eyes and without putting any strain on them, I concentrate on the mid-point of the forehead. I breathe in and out slowly being aware of the breathing itself. And when I'm really focussed, a unique drama appears to unfold within me. I must however, be sincere, patient and willing to 'accept' what I receive.

What one may *see and feel* in this state may come as a pleasant shock but one must be patient. Practice, practice and more practice, is all that's required to reveal one's real *self*.

No kidding.

STOP THE WORLD

'I want to get off'

What a fallacy! Why do we want to get off the world? Where would we go if we did get off? If 'another world' does exist, what guarantee do we have that we'll be happy there? If everyone else 'got off' this world, wouldn't the 'New World' become the same as this one?

There is no way out, no permanent escape from this place while we're living here. We have *to be what we are*, here, until our *allotted period* is over and have no choice but to pass our *allotted time*. We can do it by whining or by chasing 'material dreams' or by seeking 'the truth'

For a life free of tension, one must accept things as they are – good or bad. Enjoy good things as they come but maintain composure during bad times, accepting them the same way as one accepts the good times, without question. Good times do not last forever and neither do bad times, like night following the day and so on. We all know, some days are longer than nights and some nights are longer than days.

C'est la vie. That's life, my friend. Let's live to it's fullest, in good times *and* in bad times alike.

We can't stop the world, so why not 'enjoy the ride'.

ALL I NEED TO DO

All I need to do is just *flow* in this vast ocean of energy I call Creation and enjoy being part of it, letting happen whatever happens.

Like a link in a chain 'hooked' at both ends, like birth, death, rebirth and so on; I know the 'Creation' 'was', 'is' and 'will be', regardless of my 'coming', 'being' and 'going'.

And since, I 'was' before and 'will be' again, I am not afraid about what happens to 'me' after death. My 'real self' who is invisible to the naked eye, becomes visible when manifested in a material body, creating what is normally called a 'living being'. The death of the material body therefore, is irrelevant because it will happen again and again. If so, then why worry about what happens in life, what is 'is' and what'll be 'will be'.

And since I am part of the Source itself, shouldn't it be the Source's problem as to what happens to *me* at any given time? If everything, including *me*, belongs to the Source, then *my* worrying about what's happening seems of no relevance. Shouldn't all this be the Source's problem?

The field, the game, the players, the rules - all belong to the Source. End of story.

END IS THE BEGINNING

Ever wonder why a baby cries at birth? Have you ever seen a baby smile or laugh at birth?

Even though the baby stayed in dark and congested environment, in a very awkward position for a long time, it must have become used to it. The process of reluctant traveling through the birth canal therefore must be very traumatic for the baby. The loud cry at birth is probably due the baby thinking that it's dying whereas *we* know that the baby is actually entering a new life altogether.

Have you ever tried to move a spider or ant from the house? See how they run scared as if their end is near. But only *you* know that you are actually saving the life of the poor creature.

As discussed elsewhere in this book, we are *here now*, because we were *somewhere else before* and not only we'll prevail after the disintegration of this material body, we'll be back again and again and the life will keep on going as it has been since the time immemorial.

Could it therefore be possible, that the death of the material body may automatically lead to a new birth, back on this earth or in any other 'parallel world'?

WHAT'S IN IT FOR ME?

Seems to be the question asked quite frequently, whenever one is required to do something for someone. Some ask the question up front while others simply ponder.

And therein lies the reason of the most of our problems.

The tendency to expect a *reward* for everything we do is nothing more than a mere exchange of favors.

When someone asks us a favor, our ego gets inflated and the superiority complex takes over. The feeling of being more powerful than the person asking for favor, makes us *demand* something in return. And that makes us selfish.

The down side of such an attitude is that when we lose our ability to *help* others, we feel powerless and become miserable.

On the other hand, if we just helped people, without expecting anything in return, we wouldn't be miserable if we lost our ability to do so.

Helping others without expecting anything in return, is really blissful.

Try it; you'll be amazed.

LAST DAY OF MY LIFE

'Today is the first day of the rest of my life' means to me, like starting all over again each day. And if I spend each 'today' as my first day, I won't have time to grow up and really enjoy the life. I do not want to remain *adolescent* all my life.

How about 'Today is the last day of the rest of my life'?

To me, this means I must enjoy today to its fullest; love everything but have no attachments since tomorrow, nothing will matter to me. Friends and enemies would be the same because as far as I am cocerned, there is no tomorrow for me; so why worry.

You see, if tomorrow never comes then why should I be worried about what's going to happen tomorrow.

There would be no need to 'settle' any scores so I would be calm. I won't have any need to build an empire so I would be at peace and harmony with everybody.

I would help others without expecting anything in return because tomorrow, it won't be of any consequence to me .

I could go on, but I think you get the idea.

LET IT BE?

"But how? How is it possible in this wretched world where everyone is only thinking of himself? How can I *let it be* when everybody seems to be taking advantage of the other? How can I remain incognizant and why?"

Glad you asked. And you've already taken the first step to understanding - just by being with the book thus far.

Hopefully by this time, I have been able to impress upon you the insignificance of our *being* on this planet. All there is to understand, is the *truth*, that our coming, staying here and departing, is no more than the flash of a firefly. To the firefly it may seem an endless show of brightness but to us, it is only a *flash*.

Our *being* here is also insignificant in this *grand scheme of things* we call the universe. Think of how many millions of years our solar system, the Milky Way and the Universe have been in existence and compare that to the measly few years of our current life span. Let's remember the flash of the firefly and just *accept* things as they are. Life is too short.

There is no bigger curse than worrying about what we don't have and there is no bigger boon than being content with what we have been blessed with. Just *let it be*.

chapter 6

LIFE'S REAL NEEDS

What's in chapter 6

What is Success?
Do You Have a Goal?
Should We Have Desires?
Are You Jealous?
Bonds of Selfishness
Real Need
The Righteousness

WHAT IS SUCCESS?

How do we define success? Is it money, position, health, good family, big house, nice cars, year round golf or what?

What do we mean by saying so and so is a successful person; successful in business, in love or in career maybe? But the so-called success in a particular field does not necessarily mean real success in life.

So who is really successful? Do you consider yourself successful in life? What is *your* definition of a successful person? Are you sure you'll not need anything else after you've achieved your current goal? You probably will, and if so, you aren't really successful yet, are you?

If we could just treat everyone in this world, as part of one big happy family, we would then be working towards peace and success for all. As a matter fact, there will be no need to worry about who is successful and who is not; isn't that right?

For me, success is feeling good about who I am and what I am to others - *not what others think of me.*

DO YOU HAVE A GOAL?

At the risk of sounding passive, I must question the validity of having *goals* in life. There cannot be too many goals; achievements may be many but the goal can only be one, the *summit*, after which there can be no further goal.

And who knows what and where the *summit* really is? One may think it is different for different people; is it really? Do you know of anyone who achieved his designated goal in life and had no further desires?

Doesn't sound very inspiring, does it? Don't despair.

I am not suggesting that one should have no ambitions or milestones. I am talking about those insignificant 'goals', that literally preoccupy our daily lives.

You see, unless we are totally in harmony with ourselves, we will not be able to commence our journey to understand and recognize our 'self' and to know who we really are and what are we doing here.

And by the way, the successful completion of this journey or the current life cycle, is what I refer to as the *summit*.

The truth is that we get so involved in trying to achieve

our so called 'goals' that we tend to ignore the real purpose of our existence on this planet. I personally think that we're afraid to know who we really are and hence avoid the subject by pretending that we have no time for such *trivial* matters.

We may even step on many toes on our way to our *designated goals*. We become miserable with anxiety, while working towards our goals, and stay miserable if we fail. Even if we succeed, the sweet smell of success, also quickly evaporates and we start wondering whether the entire running around was really worthwhile. That's the time when we choose another goal and start the rat race all over again.

Why do you think they say, "Records are made to be broken".

As soon as a record is established, someone, including the person who established the record in the first place, starts working towards beating the old record. Why? Because the old *goal* must be replaced by a new one! Why?

Beats me!

SHOULD WE HAVE DESIRES?

Why not? Let's face it, we cannot live a day without having some kind of desire, no matter how small. Having desires is one of the basic human characteristics and we just can't run away from it.

So where is the problem?

It's not in having a desire but in our obsession that it must be fulfilled. We become so *attached* to our desires that we devise all kinds of schemes to get what we want losing sleep and peace of mind in the process.

We don't even question sometimes whether our desire is legitimate or not. We just want to get what we have the desire for, regardless of how many toes we may have to step upon. And therein lies the problem.

It's not the desire, but our *attachment* towards its fulfillment which causes all the problems.

Let's not become the slaves of our desires.

Whatever will be, will be; right?

ARE YOU JEALOUS?

Who, me? Never.

I only become unhappy when some people achieve what I think they do not deserve.

I don't like when they show off their riches or how smart they are.

Some people are so proud of their big houses, cars and other possessions, that they think they're great and that people like me, are small.

They waste money on frivolous things like expensive clothes and long vacations.

They have no respect for money and they spoil their children by giving them *everything*.

The way some people brag about their achievements, really turns me off.

Jealous? *Not me!*

BONDS OF SELFISHNESS

We may not want to admit it, but all the bonds of love, relationship and friendship, last only for as long as they serve our specific purpose; regardless whether the bond is emotional, financial, or whatever.

The moment the other person is of no use to us, we drop him like a hot potato. Oh, we may appear bonded outwardly but deep inside we don't really care until of course the same person is of use to us again.

There are bonds by birth and bonds by choice. If we do not get what *we think we deserve* or expect from the other person, our so-called bond starts disintegrating. We may wait for a while but it is only a matter of time when the patience runs out.

It is often heard, "I really care for so and so but he doesn't care, appreciate or understand." Well, if I really care for somebody then should I be concerned whether he or she cares for me or not? Shouldn't love be just 'love' - with no expectation of return? All bonds are just that, *bonds*. If we care for all, regardless of who or what we are dealing with, we'll have no remorse or regrets.

Happiness is feeling *unbonded and unattached* yet caring for everybody and everything.

REAL NEED

No end to our needs
We need more, and still need
But have we stopped to wonder
What do we really need?

The need is not to get
The need is but to give
The need is to spread the love
To live and let live

kanak

THE RIGHTEOUSNESS

What's true we do not see
The truth is out of sight
We need the eyes to see what is
To know what's wrong or right

To take something, is wrong
To receive something, is right
To expect is surely selfish
To accept is mere delight

To give but not to want
To care but not require
To love but not possess
To ask but not desire

kanak

MYTHS
AND
FACTS

What's in chapter 7

Belief
Believe it or Not
Faith
Diplomacy
Honesty is The Best Policy
Be Honest, You'll be Rewarded
Do Good and Good Will Happen
Don't Worry, Be Happy
Why Me?
What do We Talk About?
The Root Cause
Pride of Ownership

BELIEF

Belief: *Mind's acceptance* that a statement, suggestion or alleged fact is true; such acceptance being based on the testimony, argument or circumstantial evidence *but not from personal knowledge.*

So when we say we believe, we really don't know, *do we?*

BELIEVE IT OR NOT

We say we believe when we do not have personal knowledge.

On attainment of personal knowledge we say, we 'know'.

However, the basis of knowledge for many things, has changed over the years with the the development of new tools and new concepts. Further changes are also inevitable.

The so-called knowledge of a person, place, thing or event therefore, could also be a mere perception, that may change in time.

The only way to really *know*, is by experiencing the known then living it and eventually becoming the 'known' itself.

Simply knowing that we are a part of the Source isn't enough. Experiencing this knowledge in one's self, will set one free from all fears.

Does the word 'human being' sound familiar?

Being!

FAITH

Faith: *Mind's acceptance* that a principle as declared by someone in authority, is true.

We really do not know whether that 'someone' has the personal knowledge of the truthfulness of what's being declared.

It is not impossible to become overwhelmed when a concept is being presented in a dramatic, forceful or even in an extremely logical manner, irrespective of the reality.

We may just 'believe in' what's being declared and call it 'faith'. And we already know that 'belief' is not personal knowledge; it's just an agreement of mind to what's being presented.

If we know then we know - that's all. There is no need to rely on the declaration by others.

DIPLOMACY

Diplomacy: Skillful presentation or maneuvering of facts to get things done to one's advantage.

Note, 'skillful' or 'maneuvering' - not by presenting the facts, as they are, not even by simply telling like it is.

Indicates hidden motive, doesn't it?

Whatever happened to the reality?

It seems that using diplomacy is not exactly telling the truth, not saying how we really feel. It appears to be just an art of presentation to secure certain advantages by cleverly rearranging or twisting the facts.

How selfish!

HONESTY IS THE BEST POLICY

Does it mean any policy that is less than the best, is not based on honesty?

Shouldn't every policy be based on honesty, period?

Why is there a need to declare the honesty?

Does declaring honesty make one 'more honest'?

Is a more honest person better than the one who's simply honest?

Not hard to figure out, is it?

BE HONEST, YOU'LL BE REWARDED

·· What if you are not rewarded?

·· What if you are punished instead of being rewarded for being honest?

·· What if people don't like you because your honesty hurts someone or someone's feelings?

·· What if your honesty caused *you* hardships?

·· Should honesty be based upon rewards or should one be just *honest*, period?

Think about it.

DO GOOD AND GOOD WILL HAPPEN

" What if good things do not happen in return?

" What if bad things happen in return?

" What if we are punished instead of being rewarded?

" What if others become jealous and try to harm us?

" Would we stop doing good, if consequences are negative or would we carry on regardless of the outcome?

" Even better, isn't just being good, 'good enough'?

Doing good without expecting anything in return,
is what living is all about.

kanak

DON'T WORRY, BE HAPPY

'Don't Worry' in the above statement implies an action, and since every action produces a reaction or result, it would be a depressing emotion in this case. But really, do we have control on whether to worry or not? Do we decide that on such and such I am going worry for such and such time? I don't think so.

Worrying therefore, is not an action but is a state of mind.

'Be Happy' on other hand, sounds right because 'being' in this case, being happy, is just a state of mind, a condition that simply does not produce a reaction.

Since *being worried* or *being happy* is really not under our control, all we can do is, become witnesses to the process as it unfolds in our mind.

And if we can *be worried* or *be happy* while being *unattached* to such a state of mind, we won't have to bear the consequences of being *in* such a state.

No anxiety and no fear.

WHY ME?

Sounds familiar? How often, at the time of distress, we, in vain, ask this question?

Remember, only when things do not go our way, we seem to develop the notion that we did not deserve the failure and invariably ask ourselves "what did I do to deserve this?"

As if, we are always right and and never did anything wrong. What an attitude!

In good times, when things are going our way, do we ever ask Why Me?. Do we ever stop to think what did we really 'do' to deserve our good fortunes; things like good looks, good family and friends, good health, a comfortable life etc. etc.?

Our ego may make us take credit for our successes and achievements but the truth is that almost all of them, have been simply bestowed upon us. We do not say Why me while we're enjoying good fortunes, we simply accept them and go on with our daily lives without questioning whether we really deserve it.

Some of us even have the nerve to boast "I succeeded because I worked hard; I got where I am because of my dedication; I'm successful because I did it my way" etc.

The question of *why me* doesn't even enter the mind of most people while they're enjoying success in life.

But in times of distress, such people not only, *not accept* their misfortune, they, egoistically, challenge it's validity because they don't think they deserve it in the first place. They do not waste a single moment in blaming someone else for the whole mess. They become miserable and and complain - you guessed it, Why me?

Why don't we just accept bad times and learn to live with them exactly the way we do in good times?

Good times, bad times, big deal! All are the integral part of our life. So let's stop whining and get on with it.

Let's 'accept' everything in life without any reservation.

We really have no choice. Why fight it?

If you have to question at all, next time, try "Why not me?"

WHAT DO WE TALK ABOUT?

Have you ever wondered about the topics of conversation at parties, functions or simple get-together with colleagues, relatives and friends?

We often talk about weather, sports, movies, news, mortgages, stock markets, interest rates, inflation etc. Oh yes, let's not forget politics. And what about the jokes? All kinds - political, religious, ethnic, racial, dirty jokes, you name it. We love to put down anyone or anything, just for a laugh without realizing or caring that someone's feelings might be hurt. We just want to have our so-called *fun*.

Have we ever tried to share our feelings and emotions with others, either to look for help or to help someone else? How often have we offered to help others or asked others to help us?

If only we could find the courage to change the topics of conversation to that of a more personal nature, we'll find that many others are in similar situations with common problems.

Try it; you'll find it worthwhile.

THE ROOT CAUSE

It may sound strange but the root cause of all our miseries lies in the fact that we want to be better than others. We want to have better things than others. All of us want to be 'numero uno'. We want to win, sometimes at all costs. Everything is geared towards winning and getting ahead; meaning others will have to be left behind.

Let's not forget that in any venture, there can only be 'one' number one? Wouldn't it be more peaceful and pleasurable if we all worked in harmony trying to work for a common goal?

Is it really worth yelling at the referee or at the parents of the kid who just scored a goal? Why can't we be happy regardless of who achieved the special honor; our child or the child next door? Is there really a difference except for a temporary sensation spinning the head because *my child scored*? Oh, we could brag about it until our friends and neighbors become either sick or jealous of it. But truthfully, does it really matter to us in the long run?

Running after the trivial *successes* and the fear of failure is what robs us of the real enjoyment of life as a human being.

PRIDE OF OWNERSHIP

Pride of ownership is nothing but an illusion of being the master of a place, thing or the other living beings often addressed to as the 'property'; a feeling of being able to do with it whatever the master likes - sell, rent, trade, show off, give away and who knows what.

Little do we realize that the said property *belonged* to someone else before we got it and to someone else before that. And after a specified time, the same property will *belong* to someone else and so on. Even if somehow, we manage to keep all our property with us until death, someone is going to inherit it anyway. *You can't take it with you, you know*.

So who do you think everything really belongs to? How does *mother earth* sound? All the property, the achievements, the testimonials, even the body we occupy while on this planet, stays back here, in some shape or form.

Pride of ownership simply lifts our ego creating a false sense of superiority over the person being subjected to our pride. Unfortunately, this also creates a fear of losing the *ownership*, resulting in the loss of mental peace.

Not good, is it?

chapter 8

WHAT'S LOVE?

What's in chapter 8

Love or Duty?
Love is...
Love, Love, Love
We're a Happy Family
True Love
Baby - Friend to All
I Love You, You Love Me
Where's Evil?
Are You Really in Love?
The Truth Hurts

LOVE OR DUTY?

Duty can be defined as an act to which a person is bound by natural, moral or legal obligation. Like one's performance of the duty to society, friends, spouse, parents, children and others. Any act of care and affection towards any of these, will be something that *has to be done* and thus it may be devoid of love. Oh, we may call some of these acts as love but in reality, we are simply fulfilling our obligation towards the bond, of which we have become an integral part, voluntarily or otherwise.

Let's not confuse duty with love. Love is a phenomenon that happens and is not a condition that can be forced upon. Love is not an obligation but a state, a condition that makes us do things without expecting something in return. Anything different would simply be a trade or exchange.

Even the so-called love between spouses, between parents and children or between friends is in fact, a duty - the nonperformance of which may lead to the breakup of the bond that demanded 'love' as part of the bargain in the first place.

So what *is* love?

LOVE IS...

A phenomenon of affection and care, that affects everybody and happens naturally with no regard to any bond.

The one who is in real love, loves everybody, no matter who you are or what your affiliations might be.

Love knows no boundaries. For the one in real love, all emotions are the same regardless of the situation.

For such a person there is no difference between the lover, the beloved and the love itself; all are part and parcel of the same package.

Hard to grasp in this 'me, me' world, isn't it?

LOVE, LOVE, LOVE

To Love is an action

Being in Love is a condition

Being Love is freedom

Love, be in Love or

Be Love

The choice is yours

kanak

WE'RE A HAPPY FAMILY

We sang this with our classmates and friends during childhood. It was true then and while it's true even today, we do not behave that way anymore.

Our origin is from one source although physically we may appear separate. The eternal flame of life is burning amongst all of us and like it or not, the source of this flame, is the same for the entire creation. Our pride, ego and selfishness separate us from each other as we grow older.

If we still behaved like *we're a happy family*, we'll be exactly that - happy, and the whole world will be exactly that - our family. But are we doing that?

The world is our family - really.

TRUE LOVE

If after burying or cremating your true love, you came home and found the same loved one, sitting on your living room sofa, how would you react?

    a.   Will you rush and embrace him/her or

    b.   Will you faint or

    c.   Will you call the police?

What will you do?

BABY - FRIEND TO ALL

Ever wonder why a baby is friendly to everyone? A baby, would generally return a smile to anyone who'd make gesture to him. It is not uncommon to see a baby smile even when nobody's paying attention to him. You may even have seen babies offering a smile the moment someone looks at them. Recently in a party, I saw a two year old boy raising his arms to be picked up by whoever looked at him even for a few seconds. Some called it weird but we should perhaps learn a lesson from this wonderful child who probably felt that he belonged to all and all belonged to him.

It's a pity that as the baby grows older, he is trained to differentiate between what's his and what's not. Some parents would proudly hold a toy or something and will say playfully to the baby "This is mine" hoping to hear him say, "No, this is mine". You see, the feelings of yours and mine are now being germinated in the baby who is now learning what's his and what he must do to possess it. I once saw a father saying to his child "This chocolate is just for you honey, only for my sweet baby". Needless to say how this child turned out.

Are we falling in the same trap? Let's be careful about the impressions we cast upon our children. Let's not end up saying, "Oh. I don't know where I went wrong".

I LOVE YOU,
YOU LOVE ME

What a trade! Well, if you don't, should I still love you?

I *should*, if I really care.

If we do not get love in return and stop loving the other person, then it wasn't love in the first place - it was perhaps, just a *contract to exchange emotions*.

Think about it.

WHERE'S EVIL

I went to find the evil
No one was there to find
I looked inside and guess what?
The evil was in my mind
                    kanak

ARE YOU REALLY IN LOVE?

How strong do you think your love is? *Really.*

Do you get upset easily when someone you love, does not agree with you, or does something that *you don't like?*

Are you always telling your love what to do or not to do?

Are you always forcing your opinions and threatening to break-off, if your demands are not met?

Do you try to compete with your love or try to be better?

Does the one you love, have occasionally sleepless nights fearing a break-up?

How sure are you that your 'strong embrace' isn't choking your love?

Are you sure you're in love?

Are you sure you're not being possessive?

THE TRUTH HURTS

Yes it does, but should it?

If what's being said is true and we know that we are a part of it then why should we run away from it? Our hurt or avoidance will not change what has already happened so why fight it?

Rather than getting bogged down with the hurt why not face the situation with an open mind?

If we learn to accept the situation as it is, regardless of how painful it may appear to be; we won't be afraid anymore. The prevailing serenity might even provide enough strength for all to resolve the conflict.

All we need is the nerve to stand up to the *truth* and face it no matter who said it, and when, or how.

Stay cool and boldly face the truth; *it won't hurt.*

chapter 9

THE PARADOX

What's in chapter 9

A Lost Child
Don't Cry Baby!
Lost and Found
Will You Make a 'Will'?
Midlife Crisis
Why Don't We Get It?
Are you Content?
Getting Old, Are We?
Fear

A LOST CHILD

Think of a child in a deep forest, who suddenly realizes that he's lost and doesn't remember where his home is. The child gets overwhelmed and scared with the thought of being lost. He's so scared that rather than finding a way out of the forest, he gets busy in playing again trying to convince himself that the thought of being lost was just that - a thought.

While in the play mode, the child begins to believe that he isn't lost at all and feels comfortable with his surroundings and with the company of other *lost children*. In the ensuing confusion the child is not able to recognize the irrelevance of the play, players, leaders, followers and the surroundings until next time when the thought of *being lost* again emerges again in his mind and so on.

Even when reminded by *someone* about 'being lost' or about the 'home', the child tries to justify his attachment to the surroundings by denying the fact that he is lost in the first place. He doubts the existence of the 'home' and even challenges the credibility of that special someone who's offering help to raise his awareness. The child however, is not interested in getting out. He pretends to be satisfied with his 'play' paying no attention to the warnings about the 'reality'.

Such is our obsession with this material world. We shun enlightenment offered to us and chase irrelevant goals in this material jungle. We just do not want to get out of this jungle we call 'our world'. We make mockery of the true 'visionaries' because their views and teachings do not match with what *we believe in*.

Will we stay lost forever? Not really; because sooner or later, in this birth or in a future one, we'll eventually be able to realize the truth.

That can happen now. All we have to do is, have a sincere desire to seek the *truth* leaving our pride and ego behind. As said earlier, if our quest is genuine, we'll be guided to the right path sooner or later. It'll be then up to us to listen, learn and practice, with patience.

Getting out of the jungle is no big deal if one's determined to *get out*.

DON'T CRY, BABY!

A well-fed and dry baby, after playing with his little toys and after gazing at the surrounding for a while, suddenly, for no apparent reason, starts to cry.

The mother checks the diaper and clothes, finding all in order, she tries to calm the baby by feeding. The baby's not hungry but is still crying. The mother tries to divert the baby's attention by playing with him.

The baby stays quiet for a while but starts crying again. The doctor finds nothing wrong with the baby. Each time the baby cries, the mother tries to calm him by giving some kind of incentive - a pacifier, a toy, a lullaby - whatever. But the baby keeps on crying for no apparent reason at all.

Sounds familiar?

Could the baby be crying just like the child lost in the jungle?

LOST AND FOUND

The *lost* can become *found,* when the veil of ego gets lifted with the help of a proper guide.

As said elsewhere in this book our *attachments to* and the *detachment from* this material world, are the main reasons that prevent us from learning about ourselves. We must live life to it's fullest while remaining *unattached* to whatever is going on.

So much time is wasted in looking outwardly for the answers whereas looking within one's own self is perhaps sufficient to know the *truth.* Remember the fancy words 'soul searching'; they are not really that fancy you know; they in fact, represent what's really required of us during our current *journey.*

And once you know who and what you really are, there is no question of getting *lost* again. The journey, the path and the destination, become quite clear.

No kidding.

WILL YOU MAKE A 'WILL'?

Will you make a will if you knew for sure that you could take it all with you after your death? Would you still want to leave part or all of your estate to your loved ones? Who would be the beneficiary of your life insurance policy?

In most cases "we're doing it for the spouse and children", appears to be only an excuse to hide the greed to collect more and more. There are many who already have enough but still keep struggling to be wealthier. Some call it a challenge, some call it love for work, and some say they do it to keep busy but nobody says they're doing it for the money. The greed is safely hidden behind the excuses.

Many bequeath lots of money for charitable causes; that's good; but why not donate while one's alive and make sure it's being put to proper use? Could it be because they think that they may live for a long time; may be forever?

The greed of 'holding on' until the last minute and the associated fear of losing it all in the end, in fact, robs us from the virtue of enjoying life to it's fullest. A 'will' therefore becomes nothing but a last act of desperation because one *can't keep it any longer*.

Why not review what we can give up now for better care of others, while still keeping enough for the rest of our life? Let's give while we really can. Let's live *and* let live.

MIDLIFE CRISIS!

What a 'cop out' term!

The problem is that we don't understand the changes we experience in the late forties or early fifties. We can't seem to rationalize what's happening to us so we get worried and nervous. We think we're losing our mind whereas in fact something wonderful is happening. Read on.

To me, the so-called 'midlife crisis' in fact, is an awakening, a realization of the fact that the hidden opposite sex element in our body, is trying to get identified at around the midpoint of the average life cycle. The notion that the female element is embedded deep inside the male personality and vice-versa, is not new.

These changes are comparable to the mental and physical 'trauma' that girls and boys go through during puberty. Gushing hormones and changes in physical appearance raise havoc with the emotional balance of most teenagers.

During *midlife* however, the physical and the behavioral changes are subtle and generally non-visible. These changes and the slowing down of certain activities along with a lack of understanding of the phenomenon is what gets blamed as 'the midlife crisis'.

We can't understand what's going on and neither do our

nears and dears. The result is that we get blamed as going through some kind of crisis, apparently losing our mind, becoming 'senile' or 'old' or whatever.

What crisis? Could it be that the hibernating 'opposite element' is trying to get recognition?

It's a normal human tendency that when we don't understand something, we either try to ignore it or refute the matter altogether, hoping it'll go away. Our ego does not let us accept many things that are either unexplainable or not fully understood as yet.

In the case of *the midlife crisis*, the cause may be unknown to most of us but the effect is quite evident; and since we don't know how to deal with it and have no choice but to live with it, we become delirious and blame it on 'old age'.

Some people may understand what's going on, but they are afraid to admit and deal with this wonderful state erroneously referred to as 'the midlife crisis'.

Midlife, a time to *realize* the completeness of the human body; what a wonderful state!

Thank you, O' Creator!

WHY DON'T WE 'GET IT'?

Like a child playing outside the school, who is so absorbed in his play and the associated environment, that he is unwilling to listen to anyone about the need and the value of education. For such a child, the play is everything and nothing else matters; he will argue in favor of his actions and will try to discredit all arguments put forward in favor of the learning process.

Since this child has neither entered the school nor shown any willingness to learn, he's not going to 'graduate', is he?

At the end of the day, the child is afraid to go back home and face his parents because he wasted the whole day and 'didn't learn' a thing. Promising to do better the next day, the child returns to the playing field continuing where he left off yesterday, and so on. It may be long, long time before such a child is able to comprehend the need of school, the education and it's long term objective.

The *school of life* is no different. Most spend their entire life in the *playing field* and wonder at the end whether all the so-called achievements were really worthwhile. The promise 'to go to school' the next day, is conveniently forgotten and the life goes on with *no real achievement*.

Don't 'get it', do we?

ARE YOU CONTENT?

May be for a short while. But can you remain content all your life, satisfied and happy? Does your face emanate the radiance of contentment?

It *is* possible, regardless of the physical, emotional or financial turmoil you may be in. In fact, it is so easy that most people are not even willing to try it. Let's see, how!

Look around you; think with an open mind. You will find there are many things in your life you can be thankful for. Good things you didn't even realize that were with you all the time, ready to lift your spirit. The smile of a child, a happy face, the wonders of nature, the beauty of sunrise and sunset, a radiant full moon moving graciously in and out of clouds, a good song or piece of music - things that do not cost any money. Add to that, your good health, a loving spouse, good children, caring friends and *therein* lies the recipe of contentment. You may not have them all but *some* will do.

On the other hand, you could feel miserable thinking about numerous things you would like to have but can't. Unfulfilled dreams and unanswered prayers may be haunting you all the time.

The choice is yours, you can feel good and be thankful for

what you have, or be miserable and grouchy, thinking about what you don't have. You can be happy about your own achievements, no matter how small, or be jealous of the successes of the other people.

Yes, it is up to us to be content with a glass, half-full, or be miserable about the gross injustice done by someone, who gave us a glass that's half empty.

What 'was', can't be changed, what 'is', is because it 'is' and what'll be, 'will be'. So why not celebrate the present moment and be thankful for what we've got. If we are at peace with what we are and with all that we have at this moment, we will automatically be comfortable with whatever there is to come.

The key of accepting things as they are, will open doors to lasting contentment.

And suddenly, the past, present and the future will become no more than tiny blocks of time; expended during the unfolding of the drama we call 'life'.

GETTING OLD, ARE WE?

Well, why not? Do you know anybody who is getting younger? Can we become anything *but* older? Wiser - maybe, stubborn - maybe, disgruntled old fool - maybe, but 'older' for sure. Oh, we may be able to delay some visible signs or even some physical attributes by artificial means but sooner or later the 'good old man' will arrive with full force.

And like it or not, this body will eventually go back to the nature i.e. earth, water, air, fire and space. The 'occupant' – the soul, with its 'binder' - mind, intellect, obsession and ego, will have to leave this body for further journey.

Let's face it; once the 'occupant' is gone, the 'residence' will not survive in its present form either. Pity, we cannot come to term with this reality although we see it happening around us every day.

The worst part is that we spend too much time worrying about *getting old* and not enough time in preparing ourselves mentally to face the *final truth*. Why not prepare for our *departure* by accepting its arrival with open arms? Let it come when it comes.

I'll be *cool* when it happens and will thank 'The Creator' for the opportunity of the wonderful life I was blessed with, during *my stay* on this planet.

FEAR

A painful emotion induced by an expectation of something bad to happen or by the feeling of an impending danger.

Please note, what we call fear, is only an *expectation* or a feeling; not that something has happened, or is happening, or is going to happen for sure - just a trick the mind is playing to force us, not to think of reality but of something that *may or may not happen.*

Well, anything may or may not happen; the sun may or may not rise tomorrow, it may or may not rain tomorrow, I may or may not be alive tomorrow. We, generally, are not afraid of these matters which are quite serious, but are afraid of other things that are relatively trivial.

How sad!

Whatever has to happen, will happen; whatever will be, will be; so why live in fear? Destiny always prevails but the fear, like a virus, goes through our entire system, shakes up our equilibrium and clouds our lives with misery.

If we know for sure that something bad is really going to happen then rather than living in fear, we should be working towards averting the situation or accept it, if nothing can be done. In both cases, the onus is upon us and the fear should be of no relevance.

On the other hand, if we don't know for sure that something bad *will* happen, then once again, fear shouldn't be a factor; because, as said earlier, we aren't afraid of many other more serious events that *may or may not happen*, then why are we hung up with a specific 'fear'?

Why fail before failing or feel sick before getting sick?

After all, it *may* or just *may not* happen.

Get it?

chapter 10

FINAL WORDS

What's in chapter 10

Stop Running
The Light Within
A Different You

STOP RUNNING

We always seem to be running to do this or that. We do not seem to have enough time. Lack of time seems to be one of the most common complaints in our lives.

Remember the expression 'There aren't enough hours in a day' or 'If only I had more time' or 'So much to do and so little time?' Well, all this relates to our mixed up priorities.We really don't know what we want in life and keep running to achieve various goals essentially drawn up to meet others' expectations; goals dictated by our living standards, relatives, and the so-called *norms* of the society.

Ask those who have been running around all their lives if they are content or at peace with themselves. Ask them if they know what they really want in life; they probably won't have a satisfactory answer.

And by the way, do *you* know which fulfillment would eliminate all future desires in your life? Remember, no sooner than a desire is met or a goal is achieved, another one is lurking behind the corner and the process goes on and on with no end in sight.

So stop running, relax, and think what needs to done from hereon and why. Don't wait for a disaster to *wake you up*. Live the life as it's unfolding in front of you and soon you'll *see* what it's all about. Just be sincere and patient.

THE LIGHT WITHIN

Fortunately, once the thirst for the real knowledge starts, the attention is automatically drawn towards looking for a 'guide' who can raise awareness to the 'light' already shining 'within'.

Very rarely, it happens by itself, only a *chosen few* enjoy such a treat, but let's not despair. It has been the writer's personal experience, time and time again, that whenever a genuine *urge to merge* occurs, the help of a 'guide', becomes automatically available. There is no doubt about it.

The only difficulty is whether the 'seeker' is able to *recognize* the 'guide' and is willing to unconditionally surrender his actions and thoughts to the 'guide', in order to identify and harvest the *awareness* which by the way, is already in the possession of the 'seeker'.

And when you know, *you know*. That's all.

No explanation or justification can be given.

Pity, but that's the way it is. Really.

A DIFFERENT YOU

When you'll *understand and accept* what the life is all about, you'd be looking at the entire creation with a 'different set of eye glasses', with a *tint* of understanding and compassion. Whatever you'll do from thereon, you'll perceive it as 'being done'; the 'doer' factor will be replaced by 'being done', with 'you' being only an instrument. Once you *realize* where the thoughts come from and why you do what you do, you'll become immune to the consequences of whatever goes on.

Yes, you'll look 'different' to others. You may even be perceived as selfish, nosy and perhaps weird - one of those, who get too much involved. People may also be jealous of your outlook and may even shy away from your company. Not surprisingly, those, who *know* and are *aware* of what life's all about, are most of the time, perceived as *ignorant* simply because they're in minority.

But to these people, who are 'different' because they 'know', it will not matter as to what they are perceived as.

It didn't matter to the numerous great souls that passed through this planet over the centuries; why should it matter to you? Relax; you are in good company.

Good luck.

Chapter 10 The Journey Of Life As I See

ACKNOWLEDGEMENTS

The author wishes to thank the following, for their support, in the publication and distribution of the current edition of this book:

1. Ajay and Mini Burman, Scarborough, Ontario
2. Amar Saini, Homelife / New Star, Scarborough, Ontario
3. Dr. Anjana Modi, Ancaster, Ontario
4. Bhupendra and Nutan Gandhi, Markham, Ontario
5. Chander M. Kapur, CMA, CA, Markham, Ontario
6. D. P. Verma and Asha Verma, Montreal, Quebec
7. Dave Arora P. Eng., Delta Engineering, Markham, Ontario
8. Dr. Gargi Bhatia and Mr. Raj Bhatia, Lindsay, Ontario
9. Fred and Fabiola Moretti, Woodbridge, Ontario
10. Jag M. Katyal, B.A. LLB., Advocate, Markham, Ontario
11. N. K. and Kusum Singh, Vienna, Virginia, U.S.A.
12. Parivartan and Neeru Wahi, Montreal, Quebec
13. Rajesh and Bindu Shah, Sonush Educational,Toronto,Ontario
14. Raman and Meenu Puri, Markham, Ontario
15. Ratan and Meena Goel, Mississauga, Ontario
16. Sanjiv and Seema Marwaha, Montreal, Quebec
17. Shiam Tripathi, Markham, Ontario
18. Steven and Monika Sumra, Markham, Ontario
19. Vikram and Nina Gandhi, Richmond Hill, Ontario
20. Torie Caruso, Whitby, Ontario
21. Wayne Terranova, Markham, Ontario